Actor's I

MW00676152

This Book is Dedicated to ALL ACTORS--
Published by an Actor for Actors

The **Actor's Interview Log** is an organizational book for all areas of the performing arts, designed to facilitate the audition process as well as subsequent callbacks. It's the companion book to the **Performer's Workshop Log**.

It is a tool to aid the actor in getting to the right audition at the right time with a place to record pertinent information such as: what transpired; who was in the room; what outfit was worn; instinctive feeling about the reading; etc.

Adjacent to each interview page is a blank one for current or future notes such as change of address, postcard(s) sent, personal observations and, of course, tabloid exclusives!

Also, many of the expenses incurred in the audition process are tax deductible and can be recorded simultaneously. In no time at all, you will have compiled a compact diary of past interviews for future reference.

This information in its easy format will prove invaluable at a later date when seeing a casting person, director or producer for the same or perhaps a different project. It also gives you quick follow-up reference for thank-you notes, postcards, and God willing, a bottle of champagne!

Not only is it of value to you but, it is an inexpensive, useful and thoughtful gift for fellow thespians.

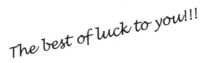

The best of luck to you!!!

- NOTES -

Postcard (dates), change of address, staff names and tabloid exclusives!

INTERVIEW DATE: _____
day   date   time

Film ___ TV___ Commercial ___ Theatre ___ VO ___ Industrial___

SAG ___ AFTRA ___ EQUITY ___ Non-Union ___OTHER___

PROJECT / PRODUCT: _____

WHERE:

CASTING DIRECTOR: _____

DIRECTOR: _____

PRODUCER: _____

ROLE NAME & BREAKDOWN:

WARDROBE: _____

HAIR & ACCESSORIES: _____

GUT FEELING / COMMENTS / NOTES

CALLBACK: _____ SHOOT DATE(S): _____

TAX & UNEMPLOYMENT INFORMATION:

Sides/Fax: $_____ Parking: $_____ Mileage: _____

Paid: $ _____ Date: _____ Commission(s): $ _____

©

-NOTES-

Postcard (dates), change of address, staff names and tabloid exclusives!

INTERVIEW DATE: _____
day   date   time

Film ___ TV___ Commercial ___ Theatre ___ VO ___ Industrial___	
SAG ___ AFTRA ___ EQUITY ___ Non-Union ___OTHER___	

PROJECT / PRODUCT: _____

WHERE:

CASTING DIRECTOR: _____

DIRECTOR: _____

PRODUCER: _____

ROLE NAME & BREAKDOWN:

WARDROBE: _____

HAIR & ACCESSORIES: _____

GUT FEELING / COMMENTS / NOTES

CALLBACK: _____ SHOOT DATE(S): _____

TAX & UNEMPLOYMENT INFORMATION:

Sides/Fax: $_____	Parking: $_____	Mileage: _____
Paid: $ _____	Date: _____	Commission(s): $ _____

©

- N O T E S -

Postcard (dates), change of address, staff names and tabloid exclusives!

INTERVIEW DATE: _____
                          day   date   time

```
Film ___ TV___ Commercial ___ Theatre ___ VO ___ Industrial___
      SAG ___ AFTRA ___ EQUITY ___ Non-Union ___OTHER___
```

PROJECT / PRODUCT: _____

WHERE:

CASTING DIRECTOR: _____

DIRECTOR: _____

PRODUCER: _____

ROLE NAME & BREAKDOWN:

WARDROBE: _____

HAIR & ACCESSORIES: _____

GUT FEELING / COMMENTS / NOTES

CALLBACK: _____ SHOOT DATE(S): _____

TAX & UNEMPLOYMENT INFORMATION:

```
Sides/Fax: $_____ Parking: $_____ Mileage: _____

Paid: $ _____ Date: _____ Commission(s): $ _____
```

©

-NOTES-

Postcard (dates), change of address, staff names and tabloid exclusives!

INTERVIEW DATE: _____
 day   date   time

| Film ___ TV___ Commercial ___ Theatre ___ VO ___ Industrial___ |
| SAG ___ AFTRA ___ EQUITY ___ Non-Union ___OTHER___ |

PROJECT / PRODUCT: _____

WHERE:

CASTING DIRECTOR: _____

DIRECTOR: _____

PRODUCER: _____

ROLE NAME & BREAKDOWN:

WARDROBE: _____

HAIR & ACCESSORIES: _____

GUT FEELING / COMMENTS / NOTES

CALLBACK: _____ SHOOT DATE(S): _____

TAX & UNEMPLOYMENT INFORMATION:

| Sides/Fax: $_____ Parking: $_____ Mileage: _____ |
| Paid: $ _____ Date: _____ Commission(s): $ _____ |

©

-NOTES-

Postcard (dates), change of address, staff names and tabloid exclusives!

INTERVIEW DATE: _____

day   date   time

| Film ___ TV___ Commercial ___ Theatre ___ VO ___ Industrial___ |
| SAG ___ AFTRA ___ EQUITY ___ Non-Union ___OTHER___ |

PROJECT / PRODUCT: _____

WHERE:

CASTING DIRECTOR: _____

DIRECTOR: _____

PRODUCER: _____

ROLE NAME & BREAKDOWN:

WARDROBE: _____

HAIR & ACCESSORIES: _____

GUT FEELING / COMMENTS / NOTES

CALLBACK: _____ SHOOT DATE(S): _____

TAX & UNEMPLOYMENT INFORMATION:

| Sides/Fax: $_____ Parking: $_____ Mileage: _____ |
| Paid: $ _____ Date: _____ Commission(s): $ _____ |

©

-NOTES-

Postcard (dates), change of address, staff names and tabloid exclusives!

INTERVIEW DATE: _____

day   date   time

| Film ___ TV___ Commercial ___ Theatre ___ VO ___ Industrial___ |
| SAG ___ AFTRA ___ EQUITY ___ Non-Union ___OTHER___ |

PROJECT / PRODUCT: _____

WHERE:

CASTING DIRECTOR: _____

DIRECTOR: _____

PRODUCER: _____

ROLE NAME & BREAKDOWN:

WARDROBE: _____

HAIR & ACCESSORIES: _____

GUT FEELING / COMMENTS / NOTES

CALLBACK: _____ SHOOT DATE(S): _____

TAX & UNEMPLOYMENT INFORMATION:

| Sides/Fax: $_____ Parking: $_____ Mileage: _____ |
| Paid: $ _____ Date: _____ Commission(s): $ _____ |

©

- N O T E S -

Postcard (dates), change of address, staff names and tabloid exclusives!

INTERVIEW DATE: _____

	day	date	time

Film ___ TV___ Commercial ___ Theatre ___ VO ___ Industrial___

SAG ___ AFTRA ___ EQUITY ___ Non-Union ___OTHER___

PROJECT / PRODUCT: _____

WHERE:

CASTING DIRECTOR: _____

DIRECTOR: _____

PRODUCER: _____

ROLE NAME & BREAKDOWN:

WARDROBE: _____

HAIR & ACCESSORIES: _____

GUT FEELING / COMMENTS / NOTES

CALLBACK: _____ SHOOT DATE(S): _____

TAX & UNEMPLOYMENT INFORMATION:

Sides/Fax: $_____ Parking: $_____ Mileage: _____

Paid: $ _____ Date: _____ Commission(s): $ _____

©

-NOTES-

Postcard (dates), change of address, staff names and tabloid exclusives!

INTERVIEW DATE: _____
day   date   time

| Film ____ TV____ Commercial ____ Theatre ____ VO ____ Industrial____ |
| SAG ____ AFTRA ____ EQUITY ____ Non-Union ____OTHER____ |

PROJECT / PRODUCT: _____

WHERE:

CASTING DIRECTOR: _____

DIRECTOR: _____

PRODUCER: _____

ROLE NAME & BREAKDOWN:

WARDROBE: _____

HAIR & ACCESSORIES: _____

GUT FEELING / COMMENTS / NOTES

CALLBACK: _____ SHOOT DATE(S): _____

TAX & UNEMPLOYMENT INFORMATION:

| Sides/Fax: $_____ Parking: $_____ Mileage: _____ |
| Paid: $ _____ Date: _____ Commission(s): $ _____ |

©

- N O T E S -

Postcard (dates), change of address, staff names and tabloid exclusives!

INTERVIEW DATE: _____
day   date   time

Film ___ TV___ Commercial ___ Theatre ___ VO ___ Industrial___

SAG ___ AFTRA ___ EQUITY ___ Non-Union ___OTHER___

PROJECT / PRODUCT: _____

WHERE:

CASTING DIRECTOR: _____

DIRECTOR: _____

PRODUCER: _____

ROLE NAME & BREAKDOWN:

WARDROBE: _____

HAIR & ACCESSORIES: _____

GUT FEELING / COMMENTS / NOTES

CALLBACK: _____ SHOOT DATE(S): _____

TAX & UNEMPLOYMENT INFORMATION:

Sides/Fax: $_____ Parking: $_____ Mileage: _____

Paid: $ _____ Date: _____ Commission(s): $ _____

©

-NOTES-

Postcard (dates), change of address, staff names and tabloid exclusives!

INTERVIEW DATE: _____
                        day   date   time

| Film ___ TV___ Commercial ___ Theatre ___ VO ___ Industrial___ |
| SAG ___ AFTRA ___ EQUITY ___ Non-Union ___OTHER___ |

PROJECT / PRODUCT: _____

WHERE:

CASTING DIRECTOR: _____

DIRECTOR: _____

PRODUCER: _____

ROLE NAME & BREAKDOWN:

WARDROBE: _____

HAIR & ACCESSORIES: _____

GUT FEELING / COMMENTS / NOTES

CALLBACK: _____ SHOOT DATE(S): _____

TAX & UNEMPLOYMENT INFORMATION:

| Sides/Fax: $_____ Parking: $_____ Mileage: _____ |
| Paid: $ _____ Date: _____ Commission(s): $ _____ |

©

-NOTES-

Postcard (dates), change of address, staff names and tabloid exclusives!

INTERVIEW DATE: _____
        day   date   time

| Film ___ TV___ Commercial ___ Theatre ___ VO ___ Industrial___ |
| SAG ___ AFTRA ___ EQUITY ___ Non-Union ___OTHER___ |

PROJECT / PRODUCT: _____

WHERE:

CASTING DIRECTOR: _____

DIRECTOR: _____

PRODUCER: _____

ROLE NAME & BREAKDOWN:

WARDROBE: _____

HAIR & ACCESSORIES: _____

GUT FEELING / COMMENTS / NOTES

CALLBACK: _____ SHOOT DATE(S): _____

TAX & UNEMPLOYMENT INFORMATION:

| Sides/Fax: $_____ Parking: $_____ Mileage: _____ |
| Paid: $ _____ Date: _____ Commission(s): $ _____ |

©

-NOTES-

Postcard (dates), change of address, staff names and tabloid exclusives!

INTERVIEW DATE: _____

day	date	time

Film ___ TV___ Commercial ___ Theatre ___ VO ___ Industrial___
SAG ___ AFTRA ___ EQUITY ___ Non-Union ___OTHER___

PROJECT / PRODUCT: _____

WHERE:

CASTING DIRECTOR: _____

DIRECTOR: _____

PRODUCER: _____

ROLE NAME & BREAKDOWN:

WARDROBE: _____

HAIR & ACCESSORIES: _____

GUT FEELING / COMMENTS / NOTES

CALLBACK: _____ SHOOT DATE(S): _____

TAX & UNEMPLOYMENT INFORMATION:

Sides/Fax: $_____	Parking: $_____	Mileage: _____
Paid: $ _____	Date: _____	Commission(s): $ _____

©

- N O T E S -

Postcard (dates), change of address, staff names and tabloid exclusives!

INTERVIEW DATE: _____
day   date   time

| Film ___ TV___ Commercial ___ Theatre ___ VO ___ Industrial___ |
| SAG ___ AFTRA ___ EQUITY ___ Non-Union ___OTHER___ |

PROJECT / PRODUCT: _____

WHERE:

CASTING DIRECTOR: _____

DIRECTOR:_____

PRODUCER: _____

ROLE NAME & BREAKDOWN:

WARDROBE: _____

HAIR & ACCESSORIES: _____

GUT FEELING / COMMENTS / NOTES

CALLBACK: _____ SHOOT DATE(S): _____

TAX & UNEMPLOYMENT INFORMATION:

| Sides/Fax: $_____ Parking: $_____ Mileage: _____ |
| Paid: $ _____ Date: _____ Commission(s): $ _____ |

©

-NOTES-

Postcard (dates), change of address, staff names and
tabloid exclusives!

INTERVIEW DATE: _____
                          day   date   time

| Film ___ TV___ Commercial ___ Theatre ___ VO ___ Industrial___ |
| SAG ___ AFTRA ___ EQUITY ___ Non-Union ___OTHER___ |

PROJECT / PRODUCT: _____

WHERE:

CASTING DIRECTOR: _____

DIRECTOR: _____

PRODUCER: _____

ROLE NAME & BREAKDOWN:

WARDROBE: _____

HAIR & ACCESSORIES: _____

GUT FEELING / COMMENTS / NOTES

CALLBACK: _____   SHOOT DATE(S): _____

TAX & UNEMPLOYMENT INFORMATION:

| Sides/Fax: $_____   Parking: $_____   Mileage: _____ |
| Paid: $ _____   Date: _____   Commission(s): $ _____ |

©

- **N O T E S** -

Postcard (dates), change of address, staff names and tabloid exclusives!

INTERVIEW DATE: _____
day   date   time

| Film ___ TV___ Commercial ___ Theatre ___ VO ___ Industrial___ |
| SAG ___ AFTRA ___ EQUITY ___ Non-Union ___OTHER___ |

PROJECT / PRODUCT: _____

WHERE:

CASTING DIRECTOR: _____

DIRECTOR: _____

PRODUCER: _____

ROLE NAME & BREAKDOWN:

WARDROBE: _____

HAIR & ACCESSORIES: _____

GUT FEELING / COMMENTS / NOTES

CALLBACK: _____ SHOOT DATE(S): _____

TAX & UNEMPLOYMENT INFORMATION:

| Sides/Fax: $_____ Parking: $_____ Mileage: _____ |
| Paid: $ _____ Date: _____ Commission(s): $ _____ |

©

-NOTES-

Postcard (dates), change of address, staff names and tabloid exclusives!

INTERVIEW DATE: _____
              day   date   time

Film ___ TV___ Commercial ___ Theatre ___ VO ___ Industrial___

SAG ___ AFTRA ___ EQUITY ___ Non-Union ___OTHER___

PROJECT / PRODUCT: _____

WHERE:

CASTING DIRECTOR: _____

DIRECTOR: _____

PRODUCER: _____

ROLE NAME & BREAKDOWN:

WARDROBE: _____

HAIR & ACCESSORIES: _____

GUT FEELING / COMMENTS / NOTES

CALLBACK: _____ SHOOT DATE(S): _____

TAX & UNEMPLOYMENT INFORMATION:

Sides/Fax: $_____ Parking: $_____ Mileage: _____

Paid: $ _____ Date: _____ Commission(s): $ _____

©

- N O T E S -

Postcard (dates), change of address, staff names and tabloid exclusives!

INTERVIEW DATE: _____
day   date   time

| Film ___ TV___ Commercial ___ Theatre ___ VO ___ Industrial___ |
| SAG ___ AFTRA ___ EQUITY ___ Non-Union ___OTHER___ |

PROJECT / PRODUCT: _____

WHERE:

CASTING DIRECTOR: _____

DIRECTOR: _____

PRODUCER: _____

ROLE NAME & BREAKDOWN:

WARDROBE: _____

HAIR & ACCESSORIES: _____

GUT FEELING / COMMENTS / NOTES

CALLBACK: _____ SHOOT DATE(S): _____

TAX & UNEMPLOYMENT INFORMATION:

| Sides/Fax: $_____ Parking: $_____ Mileage: _____ |
| Paid: $ _____ Date: _____ Commission(s): $ _____ |

©

-NOTES-

Postcard (dates), change of address, staff names and tabloid exclusives!

INTERVIEW DATE: _____

                            day   date   time

Film ___ TV___ Commercial ___ Theatre ___ VO ___ Industrial___	
SAG ___ AFTRA ___ EQUITY ___ Non-Union ___OTHER___	

PROJECT / PRODUCT: _____

WHERE:

CASTING DIRECTOR: _____

DIRECTOR: _____

PRODUCER: _____

ROLE NAME & BREAKDOWN:

WARDROBE: _____

HAIR & ACCESSORIES: _____

GUT FEELING / COMMENTS / NOTES

CALLBACK: _____ SHOOT DATE(S): _____

TAX & UNEMPLOYMENT INFORMATION:

Sides/Fax: $_____	Parking: $_____	Mileage: _____
Paid: $ _____	Date: _____	Commission(s): $ _____

©

- N O T E S -

Postcard (dates), change of address, staff names and tabloid exclusives!

INTERVIEW DATE: _____
day   date   time

Film ___ TV___ Commercial ___ Theatre ___ VO ___ Industrial___
SAG ___ AFTRA ___ EQUITY ___ Non-Union ___OTHER___

PROJECT / PRODUCT: _____

WHERE:

CASTING DIRECTOR: _____

DIRECTOR: _____

PRODUCER: _____

ROLE NAME & BREAKDOWN:

WARDROBE: _____

HAIR & ACCESSORIES: _____

GUT FEELING / COMMENTS / NOTES

CALLBACK: _____ SHOOT DATE(S): _____

TAX & UNEMPLOYMENT INFORMATION:

Sides/Fax: $_____ Parking: $_____ Mileage: _____
Paid: $ _____ Date: _____ Commission(s): $ _____

©

-NOTES-

Postcard (dates), change of address, staff names and tabloid exclusives!

INTERVIEW DATE: _____
day   date   time

Film ___ TV___ Commercial ___ Theatre ___ VO ___ Industrial___
SAG ___ AFTRA ___ EQUITY ___ Non-Union ___OTHER___

PROJECT / PRODUCT: _____

WHERE:

CASTING DIRECTOR: _____

DIRECTOR: _____

PRODUCER: _____

ROLE NAME & BREAKDOWN:

WARDROBE: _____

HAIR & ACCESSORIES: _____

GUT FEELING / COMMENTS / NOTES

CALLBACK: _____ SHOOT DATE(S): _____

TAX & UNEMPLOYMENT INFORMATION:

Sides/Fax: $_____ Parking: $_____ Mileage: _____

Paid: $ _____ Date: _____ Commission(s): $ _____

©

-NOTES-

Postcard (dates), change of address, staff names and tabloid exclusives!

INTERVIEW DATE: _____

day	date	time

Film ____ TV____ Commercial ____ Theatre ____ VO ____ Industrial____
SAG ____ AFTRA ____ EQUITY ____ Non-Union ____ OTHER ____

PROJECT / PRODUCT: _____

WHERE:

CASTING DIRECTOR: _____

DIRECTOR: _____

PRODUCER: _____

ROLE NAME & BREAKDOWN:

WARDROBE: _____

HAIR & ACCESSORIES: _____

GUT FEELING / COMMENTS / NOTES

CALLBACK: _____ SHOOT DATE(S): _____

TAX & UNEMPLOYMENT INFORMATION:

Sides/Fax: $_____	Parking: $_____	Mileage: _____
Paid: $ _____	Date: _____	Commission(s): $ _____

©

- N O T E S -

Postcard (dates), change of address, staff names and tabloid exclusives!

INTERVIEW DATE: _____
day   date   time

Film ___ TV___ Commercial ___ Theatre ___ VO ___ Industrial___	
SAG ___ AFTRA ___ EQUITY ___ Non-Union ___OTHER___	

PROJECT / PRODUCT: _____

WHERE:

CASTING DIRECTOR: _____

DIRECTOR: _____

PRODUCER: _____

ROLE NAME & BREAKDOWN:

WARDROBE: _____

HAIR & ACCESSORIES: _____

GUT FEELING / COMMENTS / NOTES

CALLBACK: _____ SHOOT DATE(S): _____

TAX & UNEMPLOYMENT INFORMATION:

Sides/Fax: $_____	Parking: $_____	Mileage: _____
Paid: $ _____	Date: _____	Commission(s): $ _____

©

-NOTES-

Postcard (dates), change of address, staff names and tabloid exclusives!

INTERVIEW DATE: _____
day   date   time

Film ___ TV___ Commercial ___ Theatre ___ VO ___ Industrial___
SAG ___ AFTRA ___ EQUITY ___ Non-Union ___OTHER___

PROJECT / PRODUCT: _____

WHERE:

CASTING DIRECTOR: _____

DIRECTOR: _____

PRODUCER: _____

ROLE NAME & BREAKDOWN:

WARDROBE: _____

HAIR & ACCESSORIES: _____

GUT FEELING / COMMENTS / NOTES

CALLBACK: _____ SHOOT DATE(S): _____

TAX & UNEMPLOYMENT INFORMATION:

Sides/Fax: $_____ Parking: $_____ Mileage: _____
Paid: $ _____ Date: _____ Commission(s): $ _____

©

- N O T E S -

Postcard (dates), change of address, staff names and tabloid exclusives!

INTERVIEW DATE: _____
                    day   date   time

Film ____ TV____ Commercial ____ Theatre ____ VO ____ Industrial____

SAG ____ AFTRA ____ EQUITY ____ Non-Union ____OTHER____

PROJECT / PRODUCT: _____

WHERE:

CASTING DIRECTOR: _____

DIRECTOR: _____

PRODUCER: _____

ROLE NAME & BREAKDOWN:

WARDROBE: _____

HAIR & ACCESSORIES: _____

GUT FEELING / COMMENTS / NOTES

CALLBACK: _____ SHOOT DATE(S): _____

TAX & UNEMPLOYMENT INFORMATION:

Sides/Fax: $_____ Parking: $_____ Mileage: _____

Paid: $ _____ Date: _____ Commission(s): $ _____

©

- N O T E S -

Postcard (dates), change of address, staff names and tabloid exclusives!

INTERVIEW DATE: _____
day   date   time

Film ___ TV___ Commercial ___ Theatre ___ VO ___ Industrial___

SAG ___ AFTRA ___ EQUITY ___ Non-Union ___OTHER___

PROJECT / PRODUCT: _____

WHERE:

CASTING DIRECTOR: _____

DIRECTOR:_____

PRODUCER: _____

ROLE NAME & BREAKDOWN:

WARDROBE: _____

HAIR & ACCESSORIES: _____

GUT FEELING / COMMENTS / NOTES

CALLBACK: _____ SHOOT DATE(S): _____

TAX & UNEMPLOYMENT INFORMATION:

Sides/Fax: $_____ Parking: $_____ Mileage: _____

Paid: $ _____ Date: _____ Commission(s): $ _____

©

- N O T E S -

Postcard (dates), change of address, staff names and tabloid exclusives!

INTERVIEW DATE: _____
 _____ day _____ date _____ time

| Film ___ TV___ Commercial ___ Theatre ___ VO ___ Industrial___ |
| SAG ___ AFTRA ___ EQUITY ___ Non-Union ___OTHER___ |

PROJECT / PRODUCT: _____

WHERE:

CASTING DIRECTOR: _____

DIRECTOR: _____

PRODUCER: _____

ROLE NAME & BREAKDOWN:

WARDROBE: _____

HAIR & ACCESSORIES: _____

GUT FEELING / COMMENTS / NOTES

CALLBACK: _____ SHOOT DATE(S): _____

TAX & UNEMPLOYMENT INFORMATION:

| Sides/Fax: $_____ Parking: $_____ Mileage: _____ |
| Paid: $ _____ Date: _____ Commission(s): $ _____ |

©

- N O T E S -

Postcard (dates), change of address, staff names and
tabloid exclusives!

INTERVIEW DATE: _____
day   date   time

Film ____ TV____ Commercial ____ Theatre ____ VO ____ Industrial____

SAG ____ AFTRA ____ EQUITY ____ Non-Union ____OTHER____

PROJECT / PRODUCT: _____

WHERE:

CASTING DIRECTOR: _____

DIRECTOR: _____

PRODUCER: _____

ROLE NAME & BREAKDOWN:

WARDROBE: _____

HAIR & ACCESSORIES: _____

GUT FEELING / COMMENTS / NOTES

CALLBACK: _____ SHOOT DATE(S): _____

TAX & UNEMPLOYMENT INFORMATION:

Sides/Fax: $_____ Parking: $_____ Mileage: _____

Paid: $ _____ Date: _____ Commission(s): $ _____

©

- N O T E S -

Postcard (dates), change of address, staff names and tabloid exclusives!

INTERVIEW DATE: _____
  day   date   time

| Film ____ TV____ Commercial ____ Theatre ____ VO ____ Industrial____ |
| SAG ____ AFTRA ____ EQUITY ____ Non-Union ____OTHER____ |

PROJECT / PRODUCT: _____

WHERE:

CASTING DIRECTOR: _____

DIRECTOR: _____

PRODUCER: _____

ROLE NAME & BREAKDOWN:

WARDROBE: _____

HAIR & ACCESSORIES: _____

GUT FEELING / COMMENTS / NOTES

CALLBACK: _____ SHOOT DATE(S): _____

TAX & UNEMPLOYMENT INFORMATION:

| Sides/Fax: $_____ Parking: $_____ Mileage: _____ |
| Paid: $ _____ Date: _____ Commission(s): $ _____ |

©

- N O T E S -

Postcard (dates), change of address, staff names and tabloid exclusives!

INTERVIEW DATE: _____
                          day   date   time

Film ___ TV___ Commercial ___ Theatre ___ VO ___ Industrial___

SAG ___ AFTRA ___ EQUITY ___ Non-Union ___OTHER___

PROJECT / PRODUCT: _____

WHERE:

CASTING DIRECTOR: _____

DIRECTOR: _____

PRODUCER: _____

ROLE NAME & BREAKDOWN:

WARDROBE: _____

HAIR & ACCESSORIES: _____

GUT FEELING / COMMENTS / NOTES

CALLBACK: _____ SHOOT DATE(S): _____

TAX & UNEMPLOYMENT INFORMATION:

Sides/Fax: $_____   Parking: $_____   Mileage: _____

Paid: $ _____   Date: _____   Commission(s): $ _____

©

-NOTES-

Postcard (dates), change of address, staff names and tabloid exclusives!

INTERVIEW DATE: _____
                            day   date   time

| Film ___ TV___ Commercial ___ Theatre ___ VO ___ Industrial___ |
| SAG ___ AFTRA ___ EQUITY ___ Non-Union ___ OTHER___ |

PROJECT / PRODUCT: _____

WHERE:

CASTING DIRECTOR: _____

DIRECTOR: _____

PRODUCER: _____

ROLE NAME & BREAKDOWN:

WARDROBE: _____

HAIR & ACCESSORIES: _____

GUT FEELING / COMMENTS / NOTES

CALLBACK: _____ SHOOT DATE(S): _____

TAX & UNEMPLOYMENT INFORMATION:

| Sides/Fax: $_____ Parking: $_____ Mileage: _____ |
| Paid: $ _____ Date: _____ Commission(s): $ _____ |

©

-NOTES-

Postcard (dates), change of address, staff names and tabloid exclusives!

INTERVIEW DATE: _____
day   date   time

Film ___ TV___ Commercial ___ Theatre ___ VO ___ Industrial___
SAG ___ AFTRA ___ EQUITY ___ Non-Union ___OTHER___

PROJECT / PRODUCT: _____

WHERE:

CASTING DIRECTOR: _____

DIRECTOR: _____

PRODUCER: _____

ROLE NAME & BREAKDOWN:

WARDROBE: _____

HAIR & ACCESSORIES: _____

GUT FEELING / COMMENTS / NOTES

CALLBACK: _____ SHOOT DATE(S): _____

TAX & UNEMPLOYMENT INFORMATION:

Sides/Fax: $_____ Parking: $_____ Mileage: _____
Paid: $ _____ Date: _____ Commission(s): $ _____

©

- **N O T E S** -

Postcard (dates), change of address, staff names and tabloid exclusives!

INTERVIEW DATE: _____
day   date   time

Film ____ TV____ Commercial ____ Theatre ____ VO ____ Industrial____

SAG ____ AFTRA ____ EQUITY ____ Non-Union ____OTHER____

PROJECT / PRODUCT: _____

WHERE:

CASTING DIRECTOR: _____

DIRECTOR: _____

PRODUCER: _____

ROLE NAME & BREAKDOWN:

WARDROBE: _____

HAIR & ACCESSORIES: _____

GUT FEELING / COMMENTS / NOTES

CALLBACK: _____ SHOOT DATE(S): _____

TAX & UNEMPLOYMENT INFORMATION:

Sides/Fax: $_____ Parking: $_____ Mileage: _____

Paid: $ _____ Date: _____ Commission(s): $ _____

©

- N O T E S -

Postcard (dates), change of address, staff names and tabloid exclusives!

INTERVIEW DATE: _____

day   date   time

Film ____ TV____ Commercial ____ Theatre ____ VO ____ Industrial____	
SAG ____ AFTRA ____ EQUITY ____ Non-Union ____OTHER____	

PROJECT / PRODUCT: _____

WHERE:

CASTING DIRECTOR: _____

DIRECTOR: _____

PRODUCER: _____

ROLE NAME & BREAKDOWN:

WARDROBE: _____

HAIR & ACCESSORIES: _____

GUT FEELING / COMMENTS / NOTES

CALLBACK: _____ SHOOT DATE(S): _____

TAX & UNEMPLOYMENT INFORMATION:

Sides/Fax: $_____	Parking: $_____	Mileage: _____
Paid: $ _____	Date: _____	Commission(s): $ _____

©

-**N O T E S**-

Postcard (dates), change of address, staff names and tabloid exclusives!

INTERVIEW DATE: _____
day   date   time

Film ____ TV____ Commercial ____ Theatre ____ VO ____ Industrial____

SAG ____ AFTRA ____ EQUITY ____ Non-Union ____OTHER____

PROJECT / PRODUCT: _____

WHERE:

CASTING DIRECTOR: _____

DIRECTOR: _____

PRODUCER: _____

ROLE NAME & BREAKDOWN:

WARDROBE: _____

HAIR & ACCESSORIES: _____

GUT FEELING / COMMENTS / NOTES

CALLBACK: _____ SHOOT DATE(S): _____

TAX & UNEMPLOYMENT INFORMATION:

Sides/Fax: $_____ Parking: $_____ Mileage: _____

Paid: $ _____ Date: _____ Commission(s): $ _____

©

-NOTES-

Postcard (dates), change of address, staff names and tabloid exclusives!

INTERVIEW DATE: _____
day   date   time

Film ___ TV___ Commercial ___ Theatre ___ VO ___ Industrial___	
SAG ___ AFTRA ___ EQUITY ___ Non-Union ___OTHER___	

PROJECT / PRODUCT: _____

WHERE:

CASTING DIRECTOR: _____

DIRECTOR: _____

PRODUCER: _____

ROLE NAME & BREAKDOWN:

WARDROBE: _____

HAIR & ACCESSORIES: _____

GUT FEELING / COMMENTS / NOTES

CALLBACK: _____ SHOOT DATE(S): _____

TAX & UNEMPLOYMENT INFORMATION:

Sides/Fax: $_____	Parking: $_____	Mileage: _____
Paid: $ _____	Date: _____	Commission(s): $ _____

©

- N O T E S -

Postcard (dates), change of address, staff names and tabloid exclusives!

INTERVIEW DATE: _____
                        day   date   time

Film ___ TV___ Commercial ___ Theatre ___ VO ___ Industrial___

SAG ___ AFTRA ___ EQUITY ___ Non-Union ___OTHER___

PROJECT / PRODUCT: _____

WHERE:

CASTING DIRECTOR: _____

DIRECTOR: _____

PRODUCER: _____

ROLE NAME & BREAKDOWN:

WARDROBE: _____

HAIR & ACCESSORIES: _____

GUT FEELING / COMMENTS / NOTES

CALLBACK: _____ SHOOT DATE(S): _____

TAX & UNEMPLOYMENT INFORMATION:

Sides/Fax: $_____ Parking: $_____ Mileage: _____

Paid: $ _____ Date: _____ Commission(s): $ _____

©

-**N O T E S**-

Postcard (dates), change of address, staff names and tabloid exclusives!

INTERVIEW DATE: _____
day   date   time

| Film ___ TV___ Commercial ___ Theatre ___ VO ___ Industrial___ |
| SAG ___ AFTRA ___ EQUITY ___ Non-Union ___OTHER___ |

PROJECT / PRODUCT: _____

WHERE:

CASTING DIRECTOR: _____

DIRECTOR: _____

PRODUCER: _____

ROLE NAME & BREAKDOWN:

WARDROBE: _____

HAIR & ACCESSORIES: _____

GUT FEELING / COMMENTS / NOTES

CALLBACK: _____ SHOOT DATE(S): _____

TAX & UNEMPLOYMENT INFORMATION:

| Sides/Fax: $_____ Parking: $_____ Mileage: _____ |
| Paid: $ _____ Date: _____ Commission(s): $ _____ |

©

-NOTES-

Postcard (dates), change of address, staff names and tabloid exclusives!

INTERVIEW DATE: _____
day   date   time

| Film ___ TV___ Commercial ___ Theatre ___ VO ___ Industrial___ |
| SAG ___ AFTRA ___ EQUITY ___ Non-Union ___OTHER___ |

PROJECT / PRODUCT: _____

WHERE:

CASTING DIRECTOR: _____

DIRECTOR:_____

PRODUCER: _____

ROLE NAME & BREAKDOWN:

WARDROBE: _____

HAIR & ACCESSORIES: _____

GUT FEELING / COMMENTS / NOTES

CALLBACK: _____ SHOOT DATE(S): _____

TAX & UNEMPLOYMENT INFORMATION:

| Sides/Fax: $_____ Parking: $_____ Mileage: _____ |
| Paid: $ _____ Date: _____ Commission(s): $ _____ |

©

- NOTES -

Postcard (dates), change of address, staff names and tabloid exclusives!

INTERVIEW DATE: _____
day   date   time

> Film ___ TV___ Commercial ___ Theatre ___ VO ___ Industrial___
>
> SAG ___ AFTRA ___ EQUITY ___ Non-Union ___OTHER___

PROJECT / PRODUCT: _____

WHERE:

CASTING DIRECTOR: _____

DIRECTOR: _____

PRODUCER: _____

ROLE NAME & BREAKDOWN:

WARDROBE: _____

HAIR & ACCESSORIES: _____

GUT FEELING / COMMENTS / NOTES

CALLBACK: _____ SHOOT DATE(S): _____

TAX & UNEMPLOYMENT INFORMATION:

> Sides/Fax: $_____ Parking: $_____ Mileage: _____
>
> Paid: $ _____ Date: _____ Commission(s): $ _____

©

-NOTES-

Postcard (dates), change of address, staff names and tabloid exclusives!

INTERVIEW DATE: _____
day   date   time

| Film ___ TV___ Commercial ___ Theatre ___ VO ___ Industrial___ |
| SAG ___ AFTRA ___ EQUITY ___ Non-Union ___OTHER___ |

PROJECT / PRODUCT: _____

WHERE:

CASTING DIRECTOR: _____

DIRECTOR: _____

PRODUCER: _____

ROLE NAME & BREAKDOWN:

WARDROBE: _____

HAIR & ACCESSORIES: _____

GUT FEELING / COMMENTS / NOTES

CALLBACK: _____ SHOOT DATE(S): _____

TAX & UNEMPLOYMENT INFORMATION:

| Sides/Fax: $_____ Parking: $_____ Mileage: _____ |
| Paid: $ _____ Date: _____ Commission(s): $ _____ |

©

-NOTES-

Postcard (dates), change of address, staff names and tabloid exclusives!

INTERVIEW DATE: _____
  day   date   time

| Film ___ TV___ Commercial ___ Theatre ___ VO ___ Industrial___ |
| SAG ___ AFTRA ___ EQUITY ___ Non-Union ___OTHER___ |

PROJECT / PRODUCT: _____

WHERE:

CASTING DIRECTOR: _____

DIRECTOR: _____

PRODUCER: _____

ROLE NAME & BREAKDOWN:

WARDROBE: _____

HAIR & ACCESSORIES: _____

GUT FEELING / COMMENTS / NOTES

CALLBACK: _____ SHOOT DATE(S): _____

TAX & UNEMPLOYMENT INFORMATION:

| Sides/Fax: $_____ Parking: $_____ Mileage: _____ |
| Paid: $ _____ Date: _____ Commission(s): $ _____ |

©

- N O T E S -

Postcard (dates), change of address, staff names and tabloid exclusives!

INTERVIEW DATE: _____
day   date   time

| Film ___ TV___ Commercial ___ Theatre ___ VO ___ Industrial___ |
| SAG ___ AFTRA ___ EQUITY ___ Non-Union ___OTHER___ |

PROJECT / PRODUCT: _____

WHERE:

CASTING DIRECTOR: _____

DIRECTOR: _____

PRODUCER: _____

ROLE NAME & BREAKDOWN:

WARDROBE: _____

HAIR & ACCESSORIES: _____

GUT FEELING / COMMENTS / NOTES

CALLBACK: _____ SHOOT DATE(S): _____

TAX & UNEMPLOYMENT INFORMATION:

| Sides/Fax: $_____ Parking: $_____ Mileage: _____ |
| Paid: $ _____ Date: _____ Commission(s): $ _____ |

©

-NOTES-

Postcard (dates), change of address, staff names and tabloid exclusives!

INTERVIEW DATE: _____
day   date   time

Film ___ TV___ Commercial ___ Theatre ___ VO ___ Industrial___

SAG ___ AFTRA ___ EQUITY ___ Non-Union ___OTHER___

PROJECT / PRODUCT: _____

WHERE:

CASTING DIRECTOR: _____

DIRECTOR: _____

PRODUCER: _____

ROLE NAME & BREAKDOWN:

WARDROBE: _____

HAIR & ACCESSORIES: _____

GUT FEELING / COMMENTS / NOTES

CALLBACK: _____ SHOOT DATE(S): _____

TAX & UNEMPLOYMENT INFORMATION:

Sides/Fax: $_____ Parking: $_____ Mileage: _____

Paid: $ _____ Date: _____ Commission(s): $ _____

©

-NOTES-

Postcard (dates), change of address, staff names and tabloid exclusives!

INTERVIEW DATE: _____
day   date   time

Film ___ TV___ Commercial ___ Theatre ___ VO ___ Industrial___	
SAG ___ AFTRA ___ EQUITY ___ Non-Union ___OTHER___	

PROJECT / PRODUCT: _____

WHERE:

CASTING DIRECTOR: _____

DIRECTOR: _____

PRODUCER: _____

ROLE NAME & BREAKDOWN:

WARDROBE: _____

HAIR & ACCESSORIES: _____

GUT FEELING / COMMENTS / NOTES

CALLBACK: _____ SHOOT DATE(S): _____

TAX & UNEMPLOYMENT INFORMATION:

Sides/Fax: $_____	Parking: $_____	Mileage: _____
Paid: $ _____	Date: _____	Commission(s): $ _____

©

- **N O T E S** -

Postcard (dates), change of address, staff names and tabloid exclusives!

INTERVIEW DATE: _____
day   date   time

Film ____ TV____ Commercial ____ Theatre ____ VO ____ Industrial____
SAG ____ AFTRA ____ EQUITY ____ Non-Union ____OTHER____

PROJECT / PRODUCT: _____

WHERE:

CASTING DIRECTOR: _____

DIRECTOR: _____

PRODUCER: _____

ROLE NAME & BREAKDOWN:

WARDROBE: _____

HAIR & ACCESSORIES: _____

GUT FEELING / COMMENTS / NOTES

CALLBACK: _____ SHOOT DATE(S): _____

TAX & UNEMPLOYMENT INFORMATION:

Sides/Fax: $_____ Parking: $_____ Mileage: _____
Paid: $ _____ Date: _____ Commission(s): $ _____

©

- N O T E S -

Postcard (dates), change of address, staff names and tabloid exclusives!

INTERVIEW DATE: _____
day   date   time

Film ____ TV____ Commercial ____ Theatre ____ VO ____ Industrial____
SAG ____ AFTRA ____ EQUITY ____ Non-Union ____OTHER____

PROJECT / PRODUCT: _____

WHERE:

CASTING DIRECTOR: _____

DIRECTOR: _____

PRODUCER: _____

ROLE NAME & BREAKDOWN:

WARDROBE: _____

HAIR & ACCESSORIES: _____

GUT FEELING / COMMENTS / NOTES

CALLBACK: _____ SHOOT DATE(S): _____

TAX & UNEMPLOYMENT INFORMATION:

Sides/Fax: $_____ Parking: $_____ Mileage: _____

Paid: $ _____ Date: _____ Commission(s): $ _____

©

-NOTES-

Postcard (dates), change of address, staff names and tabloid exclusives!

INTERVIEW DATE: _____
day   date   time

Film ____ TV____ Commercial ____ Theatre ____ VO ____ Industrial____					
SAG ____ AFTRA ____ EQUITY ____ Non-Union ____ OTHER____					

PROJECT / PRODUCT: _____

WHERE:

CASTING DIRECTOR: _____

DIRECTOR: _____

PRODUCER: _____

ROLE NAME & BREAKDOWN:

WARDROBE: _____

HAIR & ACCESSORIES: _____

GUT FEELING / COMMENTS / NOTES

CALLBACK: _____ SHOOT DATE(S): _____

TAX & UNEMPLOYMENT INFORMATION:

Sides/Fax: $_____	Parking: $_____	Mileage: _____
Paid: $ _____	Date: _____	Commission(s): $ _____

©

- N O T E S -

Postcard (dates), change of address, staff names and tabloid exclusives!

INTERVIEW DATE: _____
day   date   time

Film ___ TV___ Commercial ___ Theatre ___ VO ___ Industrial___

SAG ___ AFTRA ___ EQUITY ___ Non-Union ___OTHER___

PROJECT / PRODUCT: _____

WHERE:

CASTING DIRECTOR: _____

DIRECTOR: _____

PRODUCER: _____

ROLE NAME & BREAKDOWN:

WARDROBE: _____

HAIR & ACCESSORIES: _____

GUT FEELING / COMMENTS / NOTES

CALLBACK: _____ SHOOT DATE(S): _____

TAX & UNEMPLOYMENT INFORMATION:

Sides/Fax: $_____ Parking: $_____ Mileage: _____

Paid: $ _____ Date: _____ Commission(s): $ _____

©

-NOTES-

Postcard (dates), change of address, staff names and tabloid exclusives!

INTERVIEW DATE: _____
day   date   time

| Film ___ TV___ Commercial ___ Theatre ___ VO ___ Industrial___ |
| SAG ___ AFTRA ___ EQUITY ___ Non-Union ___OTHER___ |

PROJECT / PRODUCT: _____

WHERE:

CASTING DIRECTOR: _____

DIRECTOR: _____

PRODUCER: _____

ROLE NAME & BREAKDOWN:

WARDROBE: _____

HAIR & ACCESSORIES: _____

GUT FEELING / COMMENTS / NOTES

CALLBACK: _____ SHOOT DATE(S): _____

TAX & UNEMPLOYMENT INFORMATION:

| Sides/Fax: $_____ Parking: $_____ Mileage: _____ |
| Paid: $ _____ Date: _____ Commission(s): $ _____ |

©

- N O T E S -

Postcard (dates), change of address, staff names and
tabloid exclusives!

INTERVIEW DATE: _____

| day | date | time |

| Film ___ TV___ Commercial ___ Theatre ___ VO ___ Industrial___ |
| SAG ___ AFTRA ___ EQUITY ___ Non-Union ___OTHER___ |

PROJECT / PRODUCT: _____

WHERE:

CASTING DIRECTOR: _____

DIRECTOR: _____

PRODUCER: _____

ROLE NAME & BREAKDOWN:

WARDROBE: _____

HAIR & ACCESSORIES: _____

GUT FEELING / COMMENTS / NOTES

CALLBACK: _____ SHOOT DATE(S): _____

TAX & UNEMPLOYMENT INFORMATION:

| Sides/Fax: $_____ Parking: $_____ Mileage: _____ |
| Paid: $ _____ Date: _____ Commission(s): $ _____ |

©

-NOTES-

Postcard (dates), change of address, staff names and tabloid exclusives!

INTERVIEW DATE: _____

day   date   time

| Film ___ TV___ Commercial ___ Theatre ___ VO ___ Industrial___ |
| SAG ___ AFTRA ___ EQUITY ___ Non-Union ___OTHER___ |

PROJECT / PRODUCT: _____

WHERE:

CASTING DIRECTOR: _____

DIRECTOR: _____

PRODUCER: _____

ROLE NAME & BREAKDOWN:

WARDROBE: _____

HAIR & ACCESSORIES: _____

GUT FEELING / COMMENTS / NOTES

CALLBACK: _____ SHOOT DATE(S): _____

TAX & UNEMPLOYMENT INFORMATION:

| Sides/Fax: $_____ Parking: $_____ Mileage: _____ |
| Paid: $ _____ Date: _____ Commission(s): $ _____ |

©

-NOTES-

Postcard (dates), change of address, staff names and tabloid exclusives!

INTERVIEW DATE: _____
day   date   time

Film ___ TV___ Commercial ___ Theatre ___ VO ___ Industrial___

SAG ___ AFTRA ___ EQUITY ___ Non-Union ___OTHER___

PROJECT / PRODUCT: _____

WHERE:

CASTING DIRECTOR: _____

DIRECTOR: _____

PRODUCER: _____

ROLE NAME & BREAKDOWN:

WARDROBE: _____

HAIR & ACCESSORIES: _____

GUT FEELING / COMMENTS / NOTES

CALLBACK: _____ SHOOT DATE(S): _____

TAX & UNEMPLOYMENT INFORMATION:

Sides/Fax: $_____ Parking: $_____ Mileage: _____

Paid: $ _____ Date: _____ Commission(s): $ _____

©

- N O T E S -

Postcard (dates), change of address, staff names and tabloid exclusives!

INTERVIEW DATE: _____
                     day   date   time

┌───┐
│ Film ___ TV___ Commercial ___ Theatre ___ VO ___ Industrial___ │
│   SAG ___ AFTRA ___ EQUITY ___ Non-Union ___OTHER___ │
└───┘

PROJECT / PRODUCT: _____

WHERE:

CASTING DIRECTOR: _____

DIRECTOR: _____

PRODUCER: _____

ROLE NAME & BREAKDOWN:

WARDROBE: _____

HAIR & ACCESSORIES: _____

GUT FEELING / COMMENTS / NOTES

CALLBACK: _____ SHOOT DATE(S): _____

TAX & UNEMPLOYMENT INFORMATION:

┌───┐
│ Sides/Fax: $_____ Parking: $_____ Mileage: _____ │
│ Paid: $ _____ Date: _____ Commission(s): $ _____ │
└───┘

©

-NOTES-

Postcard (dates), change of address, staff names and tabloid exclusives!

INTERVIEW DATE: _____
day   date   time

| Film ___ TV___ Commercial ___ Theatre ___ VO ___ Industrial___ |
| SAG ___ AFTRA ___ EQUITY ___ Non-Union ___OTHER___ |

PROJECT / PRODUCT: _____

WHERE:

CASTING DIRECTOR: _____

DIRECTOR: _____

PRODUCER: _____

ROLE NAME & BREAKDOWN:

WARDROBE: _____

HAIR & ACCESSORIES: _____

GUT FEELING / COMMENTS / NOTES

CALLBACK: _____ SHOOT DATE(S): _____

TAX & UNEMPLOYMENT INFORMATION:

| Sides/Fax: $_____ Parking: $_____ Mileage: _____ |
| Paid: $ _____ Date: _____ Commission(s): $ _____ |

©

-NOTES-

Postcard (dates), change of address, staff names and tabloid exclusives!

INTERVIEW DATE: _____
day   date   time

Film ___ TV___ Commercial ___ Theatre ___ VO ___ Industrial___
SAG ___ AFTRA ___ EQUITY ___ Non-Union ___OTHER___

PROJECT / PRODUCT: _____

WHERE:

CASTING DIRECTOR: _____

DIRECTOR: _____

PRODUCER: _____

ROLE NAME & BREAKDOWN:

WARDROBE: _____

HAIR & ACCESSORIES: _____

GUT FEELING / COMMENTS / NOTES

CALLBACK: _____ SHOOT DATE(S): _____

TAX & UNEMPLOYMENT INFORMATION:

Sides/Fax: $_____ Parking: $_____ Mileage: _____
Paid: $ _____ Date: _____ Commission(s): $ _____

©

- **NOTES** -

Postcard (dates), change of address, staff names and tabloid exclusives!

INTERVIEW DATE: _____
day   date   time

Film ___ TV___ Commercial ___ Theatre ___ VO ___ Industrial___

SAG ___ AFTRA ___ EQUITY ___ Non-Union ___OTHER___

PROJECT / PRODUCT: _____

WHERE:

CASTING DIRECTOR: _____

DIRECTOR: _____

PRODUCER: _____

ROLE NAME & BREAKDOWN:

WARDROBE: _____

HAIR & ACCESSORIES: _____

GUT FEELING / COMMENTS / NOTES

CALLBACK: _____ SHOOT DATE(S): _____

TAX & UNEMPLOYMENT INFORMATION:

Sides/Fax: $_____ Parking: $_____ Mileage: _____

Paid: $ _____ Date: _____ Commission(s): $ _____

©

-NOTES-

Postcard (dates), change of address, staff names and tabloid exclusives!

INTERVIEW DATE: _____

                           day   date   time

Film ___ TV___ Commercial ___ Theatre ___ VO ___ Industrial___

SAG ___ AFTRA ___ EQUITY ___ Non-Union ___OTHER___

PROJECT / PRODUCT: _____

WHERE:

CASTING DIRECTOR: _____

DIRECTOR: _____

PRODUCER: _____

ROLE NAME & BREAKDOWN:

WARDROBE: _____

HAIR & ACCESSORIES: _____

GUT FEELING / COMMENTS / NOTES

CALLBACK: _____ SHOOT DATE(S): _____

TAX & UNEMPLOYMENT INFORMATION:

Sides/Fax: $_____ Parking: $_____ Mileage: _____

Paid: $ _____ Date: _____ Commission(s): $ _____

©

-NOTES-

Postcard (dates), change of address, staff names and tabloid exclusives!

INTERVIEW DATE: _____
                        day   date   time

| Film ___ TV___ Commercial ___ Theatre ___ VO ___ Industrial___ |
| SAG ___ AFTRA ___ EQUITY ___ Non-Union ___OTHER___ |

PROJECT / PRODUCT: _____

WHERE:

CASTING DIRECTOR: _____

DIRECTOR: _____

PRODUCER: _____

ROLE NAME & BREAKDOWN:

WARDROBE: _____

HAIR & ACCESSORIES: _____

GUT FEELING / COMMENTS / NOTES

CALLBACK: _____ SHOOT DATE(S): _____

TAX & UNEMPLOYMENT INFORMATION:

| Sides/Fax: $_____   Parking: $_____   Mileage: _____ |
| Paid: $ _____   Date: _____   Commission(s): $ _____ |

©

-NOTES-

Postcard (dates), change of address, staff names and
tabloid exclusives!

INTERVIEW DATE: _____
day   date   time

| Film ___ TV___ Commercial ___ Theatre ___ VO ___ Industrial___ |
| SAG ___ AFTRA ___ EQUITY ___ Non-Union ___OTHER___ |

PROJECT / PRODUCT: _____

WHERE:

CASTING DIRECTOR: _____

DIRECTOR: _____

PRODUCER: _____

ROLE NAME & BREAKDOWN:

WARDROBE: _____

HAIR & ACCESSORIES: _____

GUT FEELING / COMMENTS / NOTES

CALLBACK: _____ SHOOT DATE(S): _____

TAX & UNEMPLOYMENT INFORMATION:

| Sides/Fax: $_____ Parking: $_____ Mileage: _____ |
| Paid: $ _____ Date: _____ Commission(s): $ _____ |

©

- N O T E S -

Postcard (dates), change of address, staff names and tabloid exclusives!

INTERVIEW DATE: _____
day   date   time

Film ___ TV___ Commercial ___ Theatre ___ VO ___ Industrial___	
SAG ___ AFTRA ___ EQUITY ___ Non-Union ___OTHER___	

PROJECT / PRODUCT: _____

WHERE:

CASTING DIRECTOR: _____

DIRECTOR: _____

PRODUCER: _____

ROLE NAME & BREAKDOWN:

WARDROBE: _____

HAIR & ACCESSORIES: _____

GUT FEELING / COMMENTS / NOTES

CALLBACK: _____ SHOOT DATE(S): _____

TAX & UNEMPLOYMENT INFORMATION:

Sides/Fax: $_____	Parking: $_____	Mileage: _____
Paid: $ _____	Date: _____	Commission(s): $ _____

©

- N O T E S -

Postcard (dates), change of address, staff names and tabloid exclusives!

INTERVIEW DATE: _____
day   date   time

| Film ___ TV___ Commercial ___ Theatre ___ VO ___ Industrial___ |
| SAG ___ AFTRA ___ EQUITY ___ Non-Union ___OTHER___ |

PROJECT / PRODUCT: _____

WHERE:

CASTING DIRECTOR: _____

DIRECTOR:_____

PRODUCER: _____

ROLE NAME & BREAKDOWN:

WARDROBE: _____

HAIR & ACCESSORIES: _____

GUT FEELING / COMMENTS / NOTES

CALLBACK: _____ SHOOT DATE(S): _____

TAX & UNEMPLOYMENT INFORMATION:

| Sides/Fax: $_____ Parking: $_____ Mileage: _____ |
| Paid: $ _____ Date: _____ Commission(s): $ _____ |

©

-NOTES-

Postcard (dates), change of address, staff names and tabloid exclusives!

INTERVIEW DATE: _____

day   date   time

Film ____ TV____ Commercial ____ Theatre ____ VO ____ Industrial____

SAG ____ AFTRA ____ EQUITY ____ Non-Union ____OTHER____

PROJECT / PRODUCT: _____

WHERE:

CASTING DIRECTOR: _____

DIRECTOR: _____

PRODUCER: _____

ROLE NAME & BREAKDOWN:

WARDROBE: _____

HAIR & ACCESSORIES: _____

GUT FEELING / COMMENTS / NOTES

CALLBACK: _____ SHOOT DATE(S): _____

TAX & UNEMPLOYMENT INFORMATION:

Sides/Fax: $_____ Parking: $_____ Mileage: _____

Paid: $ _____ Date: _____ Commission(s): $ _____

©

- N O T E S -

Postcard (dates), change of address, staff names and tabloid exclusives!

INTERVIEW DATE: _____
day   date   time

Film ___ TV___ Commercial ___ Theatre ___ VO ___ Industrial___
SAG ___ AFTRA ___ EQUITY ___ Non-Union ___OTHER___

PROJECT / PRODUCT: _____

WHERE:

CASTING DIRECTOR: _____

DIRECTOR: _____

PRODUCER: _____

ROLE NAME & BREAKDOWN:

WARDROBE: _____

HAIR & ACCESSORIES: _____

GUT FEELING / COMMENTS / NOTES

CALLBACK: _____ SHOOT DATE(S): _____

TAX & UNEMPLOYMENT INFORMATION:

Sides/Fax: $_____ Parking: $_____ Mileage: _____
Paid: $ _____ Date: _____ Commission(s): $ _____

©

- N O T E S -

Postcard (dates), change of address, staff names and
tabloid exclusives!

INTERVIEW DATE: _____

                      day   date   time

| Film ___ TV___ Commercial ___ Theatre ___ VO ___ Industrial___ |
| SAG ___ AFTRA ___ EQUITY ___ Non-Union ___OTHER___ |

PROJECT / PRODUCT: _____

WHERE:

CASTING DIRECTOR: _____

DIRECTOR: _____

PRODUCER: _____

ROLE NAME & BREAKDOWN:

WARDROBE: _____

HAIR & ACCESSORIES: _____

GUT FEELING / COMMENTS / NOTES

CALLBACK: _____ SHOOT DATE(S): _____

TAX & UNEMPLOYMENT INFORMATION:

| Sides/Fax: $_____ Parking: $_____ Mileage: _____ |
| Paid: $ _____ Date: _____ Commission(s): $ _____ |

©

- N O T E S -

Postcard (dates), change of address, staff names and
tabloid exclusives!

INTERVIEW DATE: _____
                            day   date   time

Film ___ TV___ Commercial ___ Theatre ___ VO ___ Industrial___

SAG ___ AFTRA ___ EQUITY ___ Non-Union ___OTHER___

PROJECT / PRODUCT: _____

WHERE:

CASTING DIRECTOR: _____

DIRECTOR: _____

PRODUCER: _____

ROLE NAME & BREAKDOWN:

WARDROBE: _____

HAIR & ACCESSORIES: _____

GUT FEELING / COMMENTS / NOTES

CALLBACK: _____ SHOOT DATE(S): _____

TAX & UNEMPLOYMENT INFORMATION:

Sides/Fax: $_____ Parking: $_____ Mileage: _____

Paid: $ _____ Date: _____ Commission(s): $ _____

©

-NOTES-

Postcard (dates), change of address, staff names and tabloid exclusives!

INTERVIEW DATE: _____
       day   date   time

| Film ___ TV___ Commercial ___ Theatre ___ VO ___ Industrial___ |
| SAG ___ AFTRA ___ EQUITY ___ Non-Union ___OTHER___ |

PROJECT / PRODUCT: _____

WHERE:

CASTING DIRECTOR: _____

DIRECTOR: _____

PRODUCER: _____

ROLE NAME & BREAKDOWN:

WARDROBE: _____

HAIR & ACCESSORIES: _____

GUT FEELING / COMMENTS / NOTES

CALLBACK: _____ SHOOT DATE(S): _____

TAX & UNEMPLOYMENT INFORMATION:

| Sides/Fax: $_____ Parking: $_____ Mileage: _____ |
| Paid: $ _____ Date: _____ Commission(s): $ _____ |

©

- N O T E S -

Postcard (dates), change of address, staff names and tabloid exclusives!

INTERVIEW DATE: _____

  day   date   time

Film ___ TV___ Commercial ___ Theatre ___ VO ___ Industrial___

SAG ___ AFTRA ___ EQUITY ___ Non-Union ___OTHER___

PROJECT / PRODUCT: _____

WHERE:

CASTING DIRECTOR: _____

DIRECTOR:_____

PRODUCER: _____

ROLE NAME & BREAKDOWN:

WARDROBE: _____

HAIR & ACCESSORIES: _____

GUT FEELING / COMMENTS / NOTES

CALLBACK: _____ SHOOT DATE(S): _____

TAX & UNEMPLOYMENT INFORMATION:

Sides/Fax: $_____ Parking: $_____ Mileage: _____

Paid: $ _____ Date: _____ Commission(s): $ _____

©

- N O T E S -

Postcard (dates), change of address, staff names and tabloid exclusives!

INTERVIEW DATE: _____

| | day | date | time |

Film ___ TV___ Commercial ___ Theatre ___ VO ___ Industrial___

SAG ___ AFTRA ___ EQUITY ___ Non-Union ___OTHER___

PROJECT / PRODUCT: _____

WHERE:

CASTING DIRECTOR: _____

DIRECTOR: _____

PRODUCER: _____

ROLE NAME & BREAKDOWN:

WARDROBE: _____

HAIR & ACCESSORIES: _____

GUT FEELING / COMMENTS / NOTES

CALLBACK: _____ SHOOT DATE(S): _____

TAX & UNEMPLOYMENT INFORMATION:

Sides/Fax: $_____ Parking: $_____ Mileage: _____

Paid: $ _____ Date: _____ Commission(s): $ _____

©

- N O T E S -

Postcard (dates), change of address, staff names and
tabloid exclusives!

INTERVIEW DATE: _____

| | day | date | time |

```
┌─────────────────────────────────────────────────────┐
│  Film ___ TV___ Commercial ___ Theatre ___ VO ___ Industrial___  │
│      SAG ___ AFTRA ___ EQUITY ___ Non-Union ___OTHER___          │
└─────────────────────────────────────────────────────┘
```

PROJECT / PRODUCT: _____

WHERE:

CASTING DIRECTOR: _____

DIRECTOR: _____

PRODUCER: _____

ROLE NAME & BREAKDOWN:

WARDROBE: _____

HAIR & ACCESSORIES: _____

GUT FEELING / COMMENTS / NOTES

CALLBACK: _____ SHOOT DATE(S): _____

TAX & UNEMPLOYMENT INFORMATION:

```
┌─────────────────────────────────────────────────────┐
│  Sides/Fax: $_____ Parking: $_____ Mileage: _____  │
│                                                         │
│  Paid: $ _____ Date: _____ Commission(s): $ _____  │
└─────────────────────────────────────────────────────┘
```

©

-**N O T E S**-

Postcard (dates), change of address, staff names and tabloid exclusives!

INTERVIEW DATE: _____

day   date   time

Film ___ TV___ Commercial ___ Theatre ___ VO ___ Industrial___
SAG ___ AFTRA ___ EQUITY ___ Non-Union ___OTHER___

PROJECT / PRODUCT: _____

WHERE:

CASTING DIRECTOR: _____

DIRECTOR: _____

PRODUCER: _____

ROLE NAME & BREAKDOWN:

WARDROBE: _____

HAIR & ACCESSORIES: _____

GUT FEELING / COMMENTS / NOTES

CALLBACK: _____ SHOOT DATE(S): _____

TAX & UNEMPLOYMENT INFORMATION:

Sides/Fax: $_____ Parking: $_____ Mileage: _____
Paid: $ _____ Date: _____ Commission(s): $ _____

©

- N O T E S -

Postcard (dates), change of address, staff names and tabloid exclusives!

INTERVIEW DATE: _____
day   date   time

> Film ___ TV___ Commercial ___ Theatre ___ VO ___ Industrial___
>
> SAG ___ AFTRA ___ EQUITY ___ Non-Union ___OTHER___

PROJECT / PRODUCT: _____

WHERE:

CASTING DIRECTOR: _____

DIRECTOR: _____

PRODUCER: _____

ROLE NAME & BREAKDOWN:

WARDROBE: _____

HAIR & ACCESSORIES: _____

GUT FEELING / COMMENTS / NOTES

CALLBACK: _____ SHOOT DATE(S): _____

TAX & UNEMPLOYMENT INFORMATION:

> Sides/Fax: $_____ Parking: $_____ Mileage: _____
>
> Paid: $ _____ Date: _____ Commission(s): $ _____

©

- N O T E S -

Postcard (dates), change of address, staff names and tabloid exclusives!

INTERVIEW DATE: _____

day   date   time

Film ___ TV___ Commercial ___ Theatre ___ VO ___ Industrial___

SAG ___ AFTRA ___ EQUITY ___ Non-Union ___OTHER___

PROJECT / PRODUCT: _____

WHERE:

CASTING DIRECTOR: _____

DIRECTOR: _____

PRODUCER: _____

ROLE NAME & BREAKDOWN:

WARDROBE: _____

HAIR & ACCESSORIES: _____

GUT FEELING / COMMENTS / NOTES

CALLBACK: _____ SHOOT DATE(S): _____

TAX & UNEMPLOYMENT INFORMATION:

Sides/Fax: $_____ Parking: $_____ Mileage: _____

Paid: $ _____ Date: _____ Commission(s): $ _____

©

-NOTES-

Postcard (dates), change of address, staff names and tabloid exclusives!

INTERVIEW DATE: _____

day   date   time

Film ___ TV___ Commercial ___ Theatre ___ VO ___ Industrial___

SAG ___ AFTRA ___ EQUITY ___ Non-Union ___OTHER___

PROJECT / PRODUCT: _____

WHERE:

CASTING DIRECTOR: _____

DIRECTOR: _____

PRODUCER: _____

ROLE NAME & BREAKDOWN:

WARDROBE: _____

HAIR & ACCESSORIES: _____

GUT FEELING / COMMENTS / NOTES

CALLBACK: _____ SHOOT DATE(S): _____

TAX & UNEMPLOYMENT INFORMATION:

Sides/Fax: $_____ Parking: $_____ Mileage: _____

Paid: $ _____ Date: _____ Commission(s): $ _____

©

- NOTES -

Postcard (dates), change of address, staff names and tabloid exclusives!

INTERVIEW DATE: _____
day   date   time

Film ____ TV____ Commercial ____ Theatre ____ VO ____ Industrial____	
SAG ____ AFTRA ____ EQUITY ____ Non-Union ____OTHER____	

PROJECT / PRODUCT: _____

WHERE:

CASTING DIRECTOR: _____

DIRECTOR: _____

PRODUCER: _____

ROLE NAME & BREAKDOWN:

WARDROBE: _____

HAIR & ACCESSORIES: _____

GUT FEELING / COMMENTS / NOTES

CALLBACK: _____ SHOOT DATE(S): _____

TAX & UNEMPLOYMENT INFORMATION:

Sides/Fax: $_____	Parking: $_____	Mileage: _____
Paid: $ _____	Date: _____	Commission(s): $ _____

©

- **N O T E S** -

Postcard (dates), change of address, staff names and
tabloid exclusives!

INTERVIEW DATE: _____
day   date   time

| Film ___ TV___ Commercial ___ Theatre ___ VO ___ Industrial___ |
| SAG ___ AFTRA ___ EQUITY ___ Non-Union ___OTHER___ |

PROJECT / PRODUCT: _____

WHERE:

CASTING DIRECTOR: _____

DIRECTOR: _____

PRODUCER: _____

ROLE NAME & BREAKDOWN:

WARDROBE: _____

HAIR & ACCESSORIES: _____

GUT FEELING / COMMENTS / NOTES

CALLBACK: _____ SHOOT DATE(S): _____

TAX & UNEMPLOYMENT INFORMATION:

| Sides/Fax: $_____ Parking: $_____ Mileage: _____ |
| Paid: $ _____ Date: _____ Commission(s): $ _____ |

©

- N O T E S -

Postcard (dates), change of address, staff names and tabloid exclusives!

INTERVIEW DATE: _____
day   date   time

| Film ___ TV___ Commercial ___ Theatre ___ VO ___ Industrial___ |
| SAG ___ AFTRA ___ EQUITY ___ Non-Union ___OTHER___ |

PROJECT / PRODUCT: _____

WHERE:

CASTING DIRECTOR: _____

DIRECTOR:_____

PRODUCER: _____

ROLE NAME & BREAKDOWN:

WARDROBE: _____

HAIR & ACCESSORIES: _____

GUT FEELING / COMMENTS / NOTES

CALLBACK: _____ SHOOT DATE(S): _____

TAX & UNEMPLOYMENT INFORMATION:

| Sides/Fax: $_____ Parking: $_____ Mileage: _____ |
| Paid: $ _____ Date: _____ Commission(s): $ _____ |

©

-NOTES-

Postcard (dates), change of address, staff names and tabloid exclusives!

INTERVIEW DATE: _____
day   date   time

Film ___ TV___ Commercial ___ Theatre ___ VO ___ Industrial___	
SAG ___ AFTRA ___ EQUITY ___ Non-Union ___OTHER___	

PROJECT / PRODUCT: _____

WHERE:

CASTING DIRECTOR: _____

DIRECTOR: _____

PRODUCER: _____

ROLE NAME & BREAKDOWN:

WARDROBE: _____

HAIR & ACCESSORIES: _____

GUT FEELING / COMMENTS / NOTES

CALLBACK: _____ SHOOT DATE(S): _____

TAX & UNEMPLOYMENT INFORMATION:

Sides/Fax: $_____	Parking: $_____	Mileage: _____
Paid: $ _____	Date: _____	Commission(s): $ _____

©

-NOTES-

Postcard (dates), change of address, staff names and tabloid exclusives!

INTERVIEW DATE: _____

day   date   time

Film ___ TV___ Commercial ___ Theatre ___ VO ___ Industrial___

SAG ___ AFTRA ___ EQUITY ___ Non-Union ___OTHER___

PROJECT / PRODUCT: _____

WHERE:

CASTING DIRECTOR: _____

DIRECTOR: _____

PRODUCER: _____

ROLE NAME & BREAKDOWN:

WARDROBE: _____

HAIR & ACCESSORIES: _____

GUT FEELING / COMMENTS / NOTES

CALLBACK: _____ SHOOT DATE(S): _____

TAX & UNEMPLOYMENT INFORMATION:

Sides/Fax: $_____ Parking: $_____ Mileage: _____

Paid: $ _____ Date: _____ Commission(s): $ _____

©

-NOTES-

Postcard (dates), change of address, staff names and
tabloid exclusives!